Copyright © Gary B Lewis 2023

Published 2023

Compiled and layout design by Gary Lewis

All rights reserved. No part of this publication may be reproduced, stored in a retrieval system or transmitted in any form by any means — electronic, mechanical, photocopying, recording or otherwise, without the prior permission of the publisher / author — unless specified.

Lewis, Gary B, 1952 —

Prayer Bubbles: turning thoughts into prayers for prayer hesitants

1. Praying   2. Thoughts and Prayers   3. Meditation   I. Title

ISBN: 978-0-6455552-3-3

Digital images used and modified with permission.

Published by Gary B Lewis

Cranbourne East, VICTORIA 3977

gazzablew@bigpond.com

Prayer Bubbles

turning thoughts into prayers for prayer hesitants

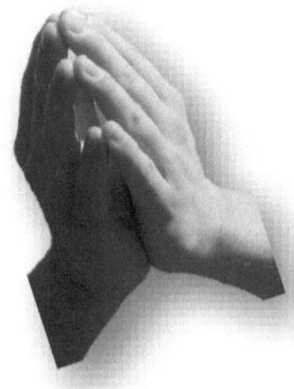

Gary B Lewis

Contents

Acknowledgments vi

Introduction.. vii

Chapter One: GETTING INSIDE YOUR HEAD 10
Chapter Two: WITHOUT WAX............................15
Chapter Three: MAKE A WISH..........................19
Chapter Four: WHISPERY PRAYERS 21
Chapter Five: SOFTER THAN A WHISPER............29
Chapter Six: IMPLICIT vs EXPLICIT PRAYER.......33
Chapter Seven: SIT IN THIS CHAIR 38
Chapter Eight: I SEE YOU.................................42
Chapter Nine: I HEAR YOU 47
Chapter Ten: MERGING PRAYER BUBBLES 51
Chapter Eleven: 'INNIE' OR 'OUTIE' 55
Chapter Twelve: IN YOUR DREAMS 62
Chapter Thirteen: UNSPOKEN PRAYERS 65
Chapter Fourteen: BUBBLE PRAYERS 68
Chapter Fifteen: OPEN-ENDED BUBBLES.............73
              SOURCES & QUOTES..................76

Acknowledgements

Firstly, I would like to thank all those people who have bought and read my previous book 'Vertically Challenged: the ups and downs of praying' published in 2022[1]. I especially want to thank those who provided feedback in terms of encouragement with such comments as "I needed to read it slowly and process the challenges presented" or "I've read it twice already!" Others remarked how God had encouraged them in specific areas or released them from past hurts.

Next, I would like to acknowledge all those people over my lifetime with whom I have had the privilege of praying with or praying for. You have taught me so much.

I would also like to express my sincere appreciation for the Bible—the Holy Scriptures—the Word of God for its truth, its rawness, and its encouragement to pray.

Once again, I am grateful to my wife Maree—my lifetime companion for 50 years—whose interest, support and encouragement and her scrutiny has kept me on track.

Lastly, I need to give thanks and praise to the Holy Trinity—Father, Son and Spirit who have taught me and continue to challenge me and empower me every day.

Gary

Introduction

In my previous book *'Vertically Challenged: the ups and downs of prayer'*[1], I wrote in a metaphoric narrative style to encourage readers who may be struggling in their praying on a variety of fronts.

Again, in much the same way, this book is not specifically presented as a "step-by-step-how-to-do-it" book on prayer, but rather, identifying the struggles we all have in praying— especially introverts and 'prayer hesitants'. In this book, I will endeavour to present some comparative thoughts and analogies on *what to do, when to do and why to do* — which in some way, overlaps with the *'how to do.'*

My preferred style (no!) actually my God-given— pedagogical style of teaching and learning has always tended towards *inductive learning*. As opposed to deductive learning —where one is told step-by-step the processes and the logical order of learning. This is the way my brain is wired —even though I can adapt to both teaching and learning in a deductive style.

So what do I mean by *inductive learning?* Well, I'm so glad you asked—actually I know you didn't ask—but I know you thought it ... right? I get very excited about *'aha moments'* of learning and discovery—whether if it is whilst reading, walking, watering the garden, watching a movie, listening to a sermon, chatting over coffee, or just sitting thinking about stuff.

As a teacher, pastor, chaplain, parent, grandparent mentor and now writer, I have always striven towards following

INTRODUCTION

the example of Jesus's teaching methodology—and leave the moment of discovery up to the listener / reader / student. Recognising of course, that there are those times, just as with Jesus, that one has to spell things out more clearly—especially when asked for more clarity or information.

My prayer is that this book will offer the reader the opportunity to enter into the inductive learning sphere—where truth and inspiration come through serendipitist moments of divine encounters. This book is presented as a metaphor for how we can take hold of our thoughts our worries, fears, wondering and concerns—and transform them into meaningful prayers.

This book is written more with introverts and 'prayer hesitants' in mind. Although extroverts can also identify with being 'prayer hesitant.' During the peak stages of the Covid pandemic we were introduced to a new term used to describe people who for some reason either objected to or were unable to get vaccinated: *vaccine hesitants*.

As alluded to in my previous book, 'prayer hesitants' can fit into one of the categories of people who say, "I don't know how to pray"; "I don't know what to pray" or "I don't want to pray".

If you can identify as a *'Prayer Hesitant'* in some way, then may I congratulate you on picking up this book in the first place. Secondly, if you can identify with any of the above categories of prayer status, then from the outset let's establish the best prayer-place to start from is: *'Lord, I don't know how to pray ... please show me.' 'Lord, I don't know what to pray ... please help me.' 'Lord, I don't want to or feel like praying right now ... I need your help.'*

INTRODUCTION

Each chapter can either be read as a stand-alone, or as connecting to previous or following chapters. You may even want to pause and employ some of the ideas presented before reading further on into the book.

So let's begin blowing some bubbles of prayer, shall we?

'We break down every thought and proud thing that puts itself up against the wisdom of God. We take hold of every thought and make it obey Christ.' 2 Corinthians 10:5 (New Life Version)

EDITORIAL NOTE:

Due to editorial issues in the first print run, it has been necessary to reprint this updated edition.

With apologies to readers.

Chapter One
GETTING INSIDE YOUR HEAD

"A penny for your thoughts?!" Have you ever been asked that question? I have often wondered why we would ask such a question. Maybe, it's because we want to get inside someone's head and assist them in expressing what they are really thinking. Or maybe, we sense that someone is withholding some information which could be a valuable asset to a situation or conversation.

Whatever the reason behind the question may be, I am also certain there would be times that you would not want to get inside another person's head and really see what they are thinking. The realisation may be just too overwhelming or confronting.

Back in the late 1960's, Walt Disney produced a movie and book about a young college student called Merlin (not to be confused with Merlin the magician!). The film was called *'The misadventures of Merlin Jones.'*[2] The movie focuses on Merlin's inventive mishaps with his design of a portable electroencephalograph machine designed for reading people's thoughts.

As he tuned into other people's internal and very private conversations—ranging from cynical remarks to

CHAPTER ONE

gossipy comments to sinister intentions—Merlin finds himself getting involved to the point of externalizing their thought processes, becoming emotionally involved to the point of intervening through a comedy of errors, and frequently finds himself spiralling deeper into trouble.

When I first saw this movie and read the book in my late teens, I was intrigued, and pondered on how I would handle my responses in similar situations of tuning into other's internal-thought-conversations. Or even worse, how would somebody react if they could tune into *my* thought processes? I think I would have been in even deeper strife!

Maybe Disney's story of Merlin was prophetically portraying what we are now seeing unfolding in the arena of neuroscience. Nevertheless, whilst converting thoughts into words—whether it be for providing instructions for prosthetic limbs or making conversation—we now know it is no longer just in the realm of science fiction or fantasy.

However, we also know from Biblical writings that throughout history, that a phenomenon of communication between the divine and human kind, has existed since the foundations of creation. God walked and talked with Adam and Eve. God communicated with Enoch, Noah, Abraham, Isaac and Jacob. Moses was considered the friend of God, King David learned to converse with the Lord as his Shepherd. These men and women communicated with God. And talking with God is what we know as prayer.

Fifteen hundred years after Noah's great flood, King Solomon was receiving some advice from his father, King David, who said this, *"... for the Lord searches all hearts, and understands every intent of the thoughts"* 1 Chronicles 28:9

(NKJV). In other words, "Be aware of what's in your head, son. God sees it."

Similarly in 1 Corinthians. 2: 11, *'For who knows a person's thoughts except their own spirit within them? In the same way no one knows the thoughts of God except the Spirit of God.'* (NIV)

And so on, with the Old Testament judges and prophets right on into the New Testament where we see Jesus–Emmanuel (God with us) even knowing people's thoughts.

'Knowing their thoughts, Jesus said, "Why do you entertain evil thoughts in your hearts?' Matthew 9:4 (NIV)

'Jesus knew what they were thinking and asked, "Why are you thinking these things in your hearts?' Luke 5:22 (NIV)

In his science fiction novel of 1955, British writer John Wyndam *The Chrysalids* (United States title: *Re-Birth*), we are introduced to David Strorm. David is the narrator of the story. He is one of a small group of youngsters who can communicate with each other via telepathy i.e. reading each other's thoughts whereby spoken words were redundant[3].

By now you are probably wondering where I am going with all this tinkering with neuroscience, science fiction and fantasy stuff and what does it have to do with prayer and praying!? And rightly so.

The image that I am trying to portray is that a thought is simply an idea, or an expression, a fear, a criticism, a complaint, a warning, an instruction or a story that originates within our conceptual brain and begins to take shape. As these embryonic thoughts multiply and gather—they take shape, forming a bubble or more accurately—*bubbles*— surrounded by unspoken words. Then as these constrained words begin to

CHAPTER ONE

coordinate into structured thought patterns they increasingly exert pressure from within ... in anticipation of escape. The result being that they pop out in the form of spoken words—most commonly in the form of statements, sentences or questions.

The most practical example of this I can give is in observing the difference between male and female communication. My wife has a thought which just seems to pop right out! Whereas for me—well, my thoughts seem to mull around internally as I process things for some time, so much so that at times I have even been known to say to her "I thought I had told you!" More often than I dare to admit, my wife with her 'pop-out' words tends to trigger off—forces me, to be correct—to bring my thought bubbles to the surface of expression.

Regarding prayer: King David was spot on when he instructed his son "Be aware of what's in your head, son. God sees it." And so, my prayer is that as you read this book, you will begin the process of learning how to take the thoughts in your head and express them to God—who already sees and knows. The purpose in emitting these thought bubbles is for our benefit rather than His. We were not created to withhold our thoughts but to express them.

The Psalmist, King David, wrote explicitly about his desperation to hear from God and to know that God actually hears him in Psalm 5:1-3.

> *Give ear to my words, O LORD,*
> *Consider my meditation.*
> *Give heed to the voice of my cry,*
> *My King and my God,*
> *For to You I will pray.*
> *My voice You shall hear in the morning,*
> *O LORD; In the morning I will direct it to You,*
> *And I will look up.* (NKJV)

Chapter Two
WITHOUT WAX

I have always been intrigued by how Stephen Hawking actually communicated once he lost the ability to talk. As I understand it, Hawking learned to use his finger to control a computer and voice synthesizer. But once he lost the use of his hands, he started depending on twitching a cheek muscle to communicate. Most computers designed for him relied on running lists of words. Whenever the cursor reached a word or phrase he wished to use, Hawking twitched his cheek muscle to select it. Then he'd go on to the next word until he created a sentence[4].

Speaking audibly is our most common method of communication. Oral language is unique to all humans—whilst it is also known that animals have their own communication methods and sounds.

Deaf people, we know communicate with hand-sign-language such as AUSLAN (Australia) or ASL (America); and deaf-blind people such as Hellen Keller (mentioned in my previous book), communicate through finger-signing into the hand of another person.

What if someone suffers a stroke or paralysis or an acquire brain injury or neurological impairment which leaves them completely unable to speak? Researchers in the area of neurological science along with technological advancements, have developed ways of converting brain waves into literal speech, thus enabling people with such conditions to communicate once again. Electrodes placed on the head are designed to measure brain activity and feed data into a 'virtual vocal tract' —a computer system designed to accurately mimic movements from the lips, jaw, tongue and larynx. Resulting in what sounds like or resembles human speech.

The possibilities are clearly amazing: technology which grants a person a second or even first chance at being able to vocalise their thoughts. In much the same way as people who are paralysed in their arms, hand or legs have learned to control robotic limbs with their brain thoughts, people with speech disabilities will one day be able to learn to speak again using this brain-controlled 'artificial vocal tract'[4].

This chapter may be beginning to seem a bit 'techno-nerdy' for some readers, but all I ask is that you stay with me on this. Now, back to praying. I wonder about people who appear to be paralysed or disabled when it comes to articulating prayers. There is no question in my mind that they have thoughts towards God—but how can they actually turn those thoughts into prayers?

After writing 'Vertically Challenged: the ups and downs of praying', I began to experience what I can only describe as a prayer drought. It's not that I did not want to pray—it's more that I could not seem to articulate what my heart and brain were thinking. My thoughts towards God seemed

CHAPTER TWO

muddled—even stuck to the point of being paralysed—so I was unable to express them out loud.

What did I do? You ask. What was my state of mind and spirit?

Was I frustrated? *Yes*

Depressed? *Yes, to a degree.*

Disillusioned? *Even more so.*

Defeated? *Well almost* ... until the Lord began to show me how to turn my muddlement of thoughts into structured prayer thoughts.

If you have read my previous book, you will already know that I have always been a vocal pray-er and have benefited from and even enjoyed the experience. I must confess here, though at times, I have pharisaically judged others who 'never pray out loud'.

This season of prayer drought has been incredibly revealing to me, as I have begun responding to what the Lord has been showing me, working through and experimenting with more creative ways of turning these muddled thoughts into meaningful prayers.

I continue to be reminded that I need to listen more intently to what God is wanting me to learn. From the wisdom of Winnie the Pooh we also learn that *"If a person doesn't listen ... it's maybe that he has a small piece of fluff in his ear."* A.A. Milne, Winnie-the-Pooh[5]. Maybe even a piece of wax.

Just as in art folklore which holds to the story that there was a term called "waxing" used at that time of the Italian

Renaissance by inferior artists who were not the finest of sculptors. They would cover a layer of clear wax over the sculpture, which would smooth the marble and hide the cracks, imperfections and pits of the marble. It would make the sculpture look perfect—free of imperfections causing the sculpture to take on a flawless surface. This was a pretence. To the eye it appeared smooth, but beneath the surface, it was false and inferior. The term 'without wax'—*sine cera*— is the same in Italian, Latin and Greek. So when an honest sculptor presented their work to the patron, they would make the statement that the sculpture was "Sine Cera" or "Without Wax." Our listening to God speaking to us should likewise be sincere—without pretence.

Help me Lord

    to listen ...

        sincerely ...

            with open ears ...

                without wax!

Chapter Three

MAKE A WISH

In John 14:17 Jesus says, "Ask whatever you wish ..." Let's compare: What do you wish for your new year? What is your birthday wish?

Ask what you wish! What does this mean?

Do you remember the rhyme?

Star light, star bright,
First star I see tonight,
I wish I may, I wish I might,
Have this wish I wish tonight.

So, does 'wish' in John 14:17 actually mean *'a wish'* or does it mean *'whatever you like?'* This phrase has always puzzled me—equating wishes and prayers. Really!

Forgive me for the Bible study notes here, but this is important enough to understand as to whether or not Jesus was advocating making wishes as part of our prayer practice.

The Strongs Bible Concordance[6] (#2309 'ethelo' ἐθέλω) defines the word used —'ethelo'— as:

- to will, wish, to desire
- wanting what is best (optimal) because someone is ready and willing to act.
- Usage as in: "I will, I wish, I am willing, I intend, I desire"

So was Jesus actually advocating for wish making?
I propose that in John 14:17 where Jesus says, "Ask whatever you wish ..." a better interpretation might be: *"Ask whatever you intend to ask for"*

The Amplified Bible Classic Edition puts it *"ask whatever you will, and it shall be done for you."* Or as the Living Bible paraphrases verse 7: *"you may ask any request you like, and it will be granted!"*

Remember the old adage: *'be careful what you wish for ... you may just get it'?* The moral being that a wish is not to be made flippantly or lightly. The same can be said of praying. Our prayers are not just words spoken or written on paper or read aloud. They come from within our inmost being—our heart. And God knows already our thoughts and we cannot fool God with our platitudes or pretences.

be careful
what you wish to
pray for ...

Chapter Four
WHISPERY PRAYERS

Picking up on some of the thoughts from chapter one, Psalm 5:1-3 is such a significant passage of scripture as it reads powerfully in whatever translation. For example here's The Voice paraphrase:

Bend Your ear to me and listen to my words,
O Eternal One;
hear the deep cry of my heart.
Listen to my call for help,
my King, my True God;
to You alone I pray.
In the morning, O Eternal One, listen
for my voice …
in the day's first light,
I will offer my prayer to You and watch
expectantly for Your answer.

And another from the New Living Translation:

PRAYER BUBBLES

O LORD, hear me as I pray;
pay attention to my groaning.
Listen to my cry for help, my King and my God,
for I pray to no one but you.
Listen to my voice in the morning, LORD.
Each morning I bring my requests to you and wait expectantly.

My observations firstly take me to the opening phrase: 'Hear me as I pray'. Some translations use 'hear' ... 'give ear to' ... 'bend your ear'. Others use terms such as 'listen' or 'pay heed to'. But the question is *"to what?"*

'As I pray' i.e. 'my words.' And then to make sure God gets the message the psalmist asks the LORD to pay attention and listen again and again with even more passionate emphasis: *'my meditation'* ... *'the cry of my heart'* ... *'my cry for help'* ... *'my groaning'* ... *'the deep cry of my heart'* ... *'the voice of my cry'*. The psalmist is desperately keen to make sure that God not only hears his cries for help, but almost demands that God answer his pleas. His focus is on the one true source of life and hope. No wonder he declares: "I will look up ... wait expectantly ".

CHAPTER FOUR

For a moment, let's consider more specifically the terms: 'as I pray' … 'my words'… 'my meditation' … 'the cry of my heart' … 'my cry for help' … 'my groaning' … 'the deep cry of my heart' … 'the voice of my cry' … 'my sighing'. I wonder that these expressions reflect such a wide spectrum of thoughts, that it is almost impossible to nail them down to one simple thought except for that of the concept of ***prayer.***

Now before you burst your bubble and go *"well der!"* Stay with me, because we all try to use words to convey something to another person, but we can still miss the most obvious word or phrase. So in keeping with the theme of this book, I would like to suggest that prayers not only are the cries of the heart or words spoken towards heaven; but they can also be thoughts or whispers.

When we think of a whisper, we often think of a secret message or something spoken that is not fit or appropriate to say out loud. And so it is whispered either to another person or to one's self.

A whisper is therefore a means of communication—a soft form of spokenness in a very light and gentle breath. Although there is a harsher form of whisper like in a noisy room—one that is the easiest way for the whisperer to get something across to another person. The whisperer would use a heavy-breath-whisper which is absent of vocal noise.

Whispering is an important but different form of communication between two or three people, whilst not to a whole lot of people at the same time unless one has access to a microphone and amplifier.

PRAYER BUBBLES

Speaking of whispering, I recall a sweet melody of a song I learned when I was young.

> Whisper a prayer in the morning
> Whisper a prayer at noon
> Whisper a prayer in the evening
> To keep your heart in tune.
>
> God answers prayer in the morning
> God answers prayer at noon
> God answers prayer in the evening
> To keep your heart in tune.
>
> Jesus may come in the morning
> Jesus may come at noon
> Jesus may come in the evening
> So keep you heart in tune.

The first two stanzas of 'Whisper a Prayer'[7] mentioned in particular are simple yet firmly based on scripture (Psalm 55:16-17). *As for me, I call to God, and the LORD saves me. Evening, morning and noon. I cry out in distress, and he hears my voice.*

To keep this thought in context, on the next two pages, I have paraphrased two sections of Psalm 55:1-8. Verses 1-8 and then 16-23. Note: God speaks in bold text not because it is loud but just to distinguish it from the pray-er's praying.

CHAPTER FOUR

I know you are listening God
Please don't ignore me.
Hear my thoughts
I need you to answer !
You know that it is my thoughts which really trouble me —
they distraught me.
I hear my thoughts inside my head
They have become my enemy from within.
Even when I look in the mirror I see those staring eyes
looking so wicked!
Those thoughts and stares bring so much suffering to my
soul — their anger from inside of me reviles me.
My heart — my mind, my emotions, my soul is in so much
anguish inside of me, that I feel like ending it all myself to
the point of death.
Fearful thoughts and physical trembling of my body seem
to have taken over my life — I am so horribly
overwhelmed.
How many times have you heard me say: "Oh that I had
wings, so that I could fly away and escape!"?

"Where would you go?" *you ask — ah, now I know you are*
listening!
I would flee far away — stay where there is no one else —
find a place of seclusion and shelter — far from this place
of tempest and torment!

[You might like to paraphrase verses 9-15 yourself sometime.]

PRAYER BUBBLES

Vs 16-23

Thank you for the many times I have called to you God and you have come to my rescue — whether it be in the evening, the morning or at noon. God, I know you are there and I know that you hear the distress of my thoughts and words.
You have rescued me before from my enemies — both internal and external — as they continually try to bring me down.
At this point, I STOP and TAKE A BREATH ... what's this ... a new thought?

Listen

Breathe

Feel that heartbeat.

That's God's sustaining energy — He will never let you fall. As long as you 'cast [throw the whole weight of] all you cares on Him'.**

"Your enemies within and without will not win."

That's it God! I will continue to trust in you!

** *(1 Peter 5:7).*

If you have never read the Psalms like this before, then you may have found this Psalm fairly confronting or depressing.

CHAPTER FOUR

However, we cannot help but recognise the transitional intensity from the whispering to the desperate screaming in this Psalm.

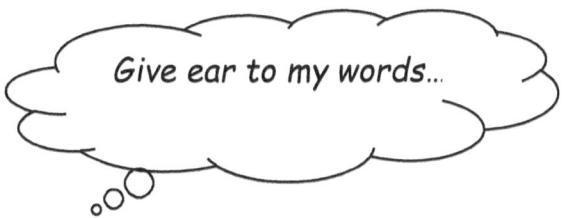

As we begin to draw this chapter to a close, just the simple display of the above thought-bubble somehow seems to give structure, substance and added meaning to the Psalmist's prayer ... so too ... you and I can thought-bubble our prayers to the Lord.

So let's take a few moments ... and look back a few pages and re-read Psalm 5:1-3. See how easy it is to envisage David's prayer bubble? Now, put this book down and open your Bible or Bible App and also consider Psalm 13:1-6 and Psalm 19:14. See the bubbles!

Blow on them
with your own
whispery breath

Now, take a notebook or whiteboard or whatever you can scribble on, and draw your own thought bubble and speak/write your prayer thoughts.

Before leaving this topic, someone might be thinking *"Yeah, but my prayer bubbles keep hitting the ceiling, burst and go nowhere or they seem to disappear immediately! So what's the point in praying?"*

Great question!

My response to that question is to ask another: *is your faith shaped by the contents of your prayer bubble? Are you more concerned about your words and needs? Or ... is your faith actually in the one to whom it is being directed — the One who hears — the Lord of grace and mercy — the Faithful One?*

In other words, we need to shift our focus from the little (i) ... me, myself and I, onto the big (I) ... the one who is the great I AM, the Word of truth ...

trusting in His will ...
in His way ...
in His time.

Chapter Five

SOFTER THAN A WHISPER

In the previous chapter we considered whispery prayers. You may ask "What could be softer than a whisper?" Without wanting to make things too scientific, my simple answer to that question would be — *a breath*. The power of breath is amazing — immeasurably so. I would also venture to add ... and even more powerful than a whisper!

The Greek word for breath is *pneuma,* We get our English words *pneumatic and pneumonia* from this Greek word. *Ruach* is the Hebrew word used in scripture for the breath of God. It is wind, Spirit, life. It's not so much a physical force but an essence—God's essence that sustains life. It's sometimes also translated as Spirit of God, such as in Genesis chapter 1.

When my brother Rodney (born deaf) was being taught to speak and pronounce words correctly at kindergarten, he was taught to lipread. In order to pronounce the sound 'ff', the teacher would hold up a feather and gently blow a soft breath to make the feather move. She would hold her lips in the correct position and gently say the sound for 'ff' — and then the word 'feather'. By this, she was indicating not only the correct mouth formation of the sound, but also identifying the name of the object. The children would each then hold the feather and repeat the process of learning.

Another reason I suggest that the softness of a breath is amazing is when someone is unconscious, with a pulse that is hard to detect. I have heard it said that a mirror can be held up to their nose or mouth of the unconscious person to see if a soft mist of air is detectable on the surface of the glass. (Or maybe this only happens in the movies!)

We tend to take our breath for granted too often I think, and yet my suggestion is that even as you read this book, you have not actually been aware of your own breathing.

Prayer is just like a breath.

Without breath we would die and yet we are not conscious of its presence. Psalm 46:1 says that *'God is our refuge and strength. A very present help in times of trouble'*.

At this point, I would like to introduce you to the concept of a 'whisper phone'. You read that correctly — a 'whisper phone'. It is not a microphone or a megaphone — although it can amplify sound. It is not a telephone — although it can be used to communicate.

Look at the picture on the next page:

CHAPTER FIVE

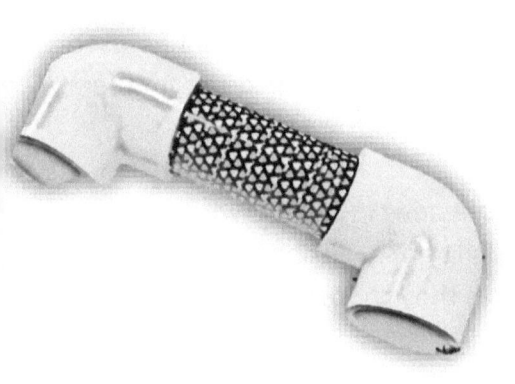

This is a 'whisper phone' made of *PVC vacuum pipe. Total length 180mm - length 105mm - 40mm bend - pipe 35mm diam.* Holding up the 'whisper phone' to your mouth and ear like an old-fashioned telephone handset; you can whisper something softly into the mouthpiece that only you can hear — actually you and God!

<u>DISCLAIMER</u>: never shout into the mouthpiece with the other end to yours or anyone's ear!

In educational settings, these 'whisper phones' are used to help children to quietly check their own spelling without disturbing others nearby. Or even for those children who need to continue to read out loud. Yours truly has used the 'whisper phone' in small group settings for children to whisper their fears, or their goals when they might feel embarrassed or reluctant to share with the group. By using a 'whisper phone', they hear their own voice in their ear saying something would otherwise be unutterable for them.

I have also heard of children who have had a tendency towards selective mutism.* The 'whisper phone' can be used to encourage them to whisper to themselves, in order for them to become familiar with their own breathy voice.

> * Simple definition of selective mutism is where someone has the capability of speaking out loud, but in certain circumstances they choose not to.

On this issue of selective mutism, I have come to recognise that there are adults who display this same behaviour when it comes to praying within a group. I am not saying that selective mutism in any situation is wrong, but suffice to say that it exists. I also believe that it is helpful for the individual to acknowledge this phenomenon. I would also go further to suggest that with professional guidance or wise pastoral counseling, they may be able to uncover the source and reason for such, with a view to releasing them from its hold over them. My observations and learning experience indicates that selective mutism is often related to some form of trauma experienced or witnessed firsthand.

If you decide to make your own 'whisper phone', then you can use it as a discreet way of praying out loud but in a whisper at the same time. You will hear yourself praying, but more importantly the Lord will hear. This little tool may be very useful for people who like to pray out loud, but due to their living circumstances e.g. living with non-believers in the house—this 'whisper phone' can provide that much needed outlet of spoken prayer.

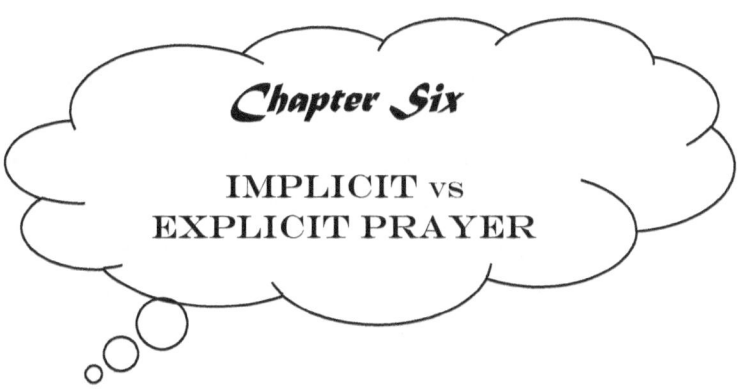

Chapter Six

IMPLICIT vs EXPLICIT PRAYER

"What is an implicit prayer?" you ask. May I suggest that an implicit prayer is a prayer which is not asking anything specific, but rather offers acknowledgement of God's sovereignty and mankind's plight.

Consider if you will, Psalm 62 which begins with *'My soul finds rest in God alone. He alone is my rock and my salvation; he is my fortress, I will never be shaken ...'* and concludes with *'you, O God, are strong, and that you, O Lord, are loving. Surely you will reward each person according to what he has done.'*

The verses in-between are more or less exhortations to the reader to maintain their focus on God alone.

This Psalm does not ask anything specifically of God, but by implication is an appeal to God to uphold his people. Whereas the next Psalm, 63, is more of a expression of longing for God and his protection.

In Psalm 62: 11 the writer, David clearly states "*I heard*"; and in Psalm 63: 2 he states, "*I have seen*".

Implicit—i.e. by implication—both Psalms are prayers. Yet by contrast in Psalm 64, David *explicitly* expresses his prayer "Hear me, O God" verse 1. "Hide me ... " verse 2. But then verses 7-10, he *implicitly* declares that "God will help his people".

At the risk of showing up my lack of Biblical knowledge and wordsmithing skills, I simply want to make the point that if the Psalmist can converse with God both implicitly as well as explicitly, then so we too can learn to exercise both forms of approaching God in prayer. As far as I am aware, no one has ever tried to define implicit prayer—so I know I am taking a big risk of being misunderstood or even considered heretical. However, if we look closely at the dictionary definition of both implicit and explicit with examples, then hopefully we can better understand the difference between the two types of prayer conversation.

The adjective *explicit* describes something that has been expressed directly. For example, saying *'We gave them explicit instructions'* means that the instructions were stated in detail. Something that's described as *explicit* does not leave anything up to interpretation.

By contrast, the adjective *implicit* describes something that has been *implied*—meaning it has been suggested or hinted at but not actually directly stated or expressed. For example, saying *'We had an implicit agreement'* means that an agreement was implied but never actually stated or written down.

These senses of *explicit* and *implicit* are direct opposites. Consider the difference between these two statements:
1. **Don't press that button—it will give you an electric shock.**
2. *I wouldn't press that button if I were you.*

CHAPTER SIX

Statement 1 is an *explicit* warning. The speaker is clearly and directly telling you not to press the button and what will happen if you do. Statement 2 is an *implicit* warning. The speaker isn't outright telling you not to press the button, nor do they say what exactly will happen if you. Rather, they are <u>*insinuating*</u>—implying, hinting—that something bad will happen if you press the button.

Directly related to *explicit* is the verb *explicate*, which means the same thing as explain. On the other hand, *implicit* is related to the verb *imply*, meaning "to suggest something without saying it." [8]

We can apply the same criteria to prayer. Are you an implicit pray-er or an explicit pray-er? Are your requests implied, or are they clearly and specifically expressed? "But what is an implicit prayer?" you rightly ask. By definition ... it is a prayer that is implied or is non-specific. It is generic as in one size fits all. Let me quote from my previous book, chapter 22:

> 'Many children are taught — or at least used to be taught — simple prayers like 'God bless mummy. God bless daddy. God bless grandma' etc. I recall teaching year four students in a Christian School in the early 1980's. At the start of each day we would have a special devotional time, which included praying for any needs that the children wanted to share. To my amazement a number of children prayed something like: "Dear Lord, please bless my grandpa." Or "Lord, we pray for Mr Roberts." I found myself thinking things like "Yes, but how do you want God to bless your grandpa? And what exactly are you praying that God

will do for Mr Roberts?" And yet, I know that these were childlike prayers offered in childlike faith.
Over the years, as these children have grown into adulthood, I have often wondered how many of them have continued this simple method as their prayer style. 'God bless our church. God bless my business. God bless our nation.' What does this mean anyway? Does it actually mean 'have favour upon'? Or is it just another cliché?'

Throughout my previous book, I *explicitly* encouraged readers to pray scripturally i.e. reminding God of what His Word says and therefore praying from a position of victory. By contrast, implicitly praying tends more towards wishful thinking or dare I say ... praying without a specific purpose.

Elsewhere, I provided different examples of being more specific and explicitly praying in line with scripture:

Needing financial assistance? Once again praying in line with scripture and faith who God says He is: "Lord, it says in the Bible that You are Jehovah Jireh — the Lord who supplies and provides. And scripture also says that You own the cattle on a thousand hills as well as the wealth in every mine. Your Word reminds me that You will provide for all my needs, according to Your riches in Christ Jesus. Lord, I need You to come through with some provision of finance right now and I thank You in advance for how You will meet this need. Amen."

CHAPTER SIX

An even more explicit prayer would be go to further to ask the Lord specifically for the required amount of money or goods. Scripture actually says we can boldly approach the throne of grace [Heb 4:16], and reminds us that we have not because we ask not [James 4:2-3]

Now I can just hear someone reeling out of their chair, *"You can't dictate to God!"* And they would right of course. But even Jesus encouraged people to be explicit. In Luke 14 we read of the blind beggar:

> *"Jesus stopped and directed that the man be brought to Him. When he had been brought near, Jesus asked him, 41"What do you want Me to do for you?" "Lord," he said, "let me see again." 42"Receive your sight!" Jesus replied. "Your faith has healed you."...*
>
> *Berean Standard Bible*

So ... are you an implicit pray-er or an explicit pray-er? Do you imply your requests of the Lord, or do you clearly and specifically express your thoughts and requests to Him? From now on as you pray, be aware of the words you use. Again, I am not saying one is better than the other, but rather, it is helpful for us to be aware of our personal bias in praying. From my experience, I have come to appreciate that both implicit and explicit praying work hand-in-hand. The implicit part is more about the use of scripture in reminding God of his promises and the explicit part is asking God directly and specifically for his provision.

Chapter Seven
SIT IN THIS CHAIR

In his book, '*2 CHAIRS – the secret that changes everything*'[9], Bob Beaudine sets a scene which is similar to my campfire setting described in chapter 24 of my previous book. In his book, Beaudine also proposes three questions to ask yourself, when sitting at your '2 chairs'.

These three questions are simply profound—by which I mean simple yet profound. Since having read the '2 CHAIRS' book, I have had many opportunities to share these questions with a number of people who have talked about the difficult situations they have been facing. With Bob's permission, I would like to share these three questions with you here, whilst endeavouring to stay on track with the theme of this book.

Picture yourself having coffee or a cool drink at a table set for two—although you are the only person seated at the table. You find yourself pondering about a certain situation—set of circumstances—a medical diagnosis. Something that has caught you off guard or a mounting worry of concern.

Sipping your drink, a thought suddenly pops into your head as if it were spoken from the other seat.

CHAPTER SEVEN

> *You know [your name], nothing takes me by surprise! I am fully aware of the situation you are pondering right now!*

Stunned! You almost spill your coffee and you look around to see if anyone is looking at you. You even glance behind you to see if there is a ventriloquist sitting nearby.

Nope!

After you compose yourself, catch your breath, and lick the cappuccino froth from your upper lip, your own inner voice responds with something like:

> *Only God would know what I'm facing right now!*

You take another sip of your drink and as you swallow—there it is again. Half question-half statement.

> *You do know that nothing is impossible for me don't you [your name]? Do you think your problem is too big for me to handle?*

PRAYER BUBBLES

Taken aback again, this time you spill of few drops of coffee down your front, and you look around embarrassingly. Immediately, your inner voice defends:

> *Only God could solve this problem — well actually I'm not even sure of that! But hang on! If God is all-powerful and all-knowing as well as being ever present, then I guess that my situation is not too big for Him to work out!*

You try to mop your shirt, and gather yourself together—after all this is fairly disturbing stuff! Deciding to finish your coffee as quickly as possible to avoid any more mishaps, you take one last gulp. And as you are about to place your cup down on the table, then the voice comes again causing you to actually drop the cup, almost breaking it!

> **You do know [your name], I have a plan for you don't you? Plans for good and not for harm. If you believe that [your name], then all you have to do right now is to ask me to show you what to do. Ask me ... seek me ... knock on my door. I will show you, lead you and open up the way for you to move forward. Trust me ... I know!**

CHAPTER SEVEN

Ok, by now you are probably wondering what the original three questions were in the 2 CHAIRS book. Plain and simple, here they are:

Q1. Does God know about this situation?
Q2. Is this situation too big for God to handle?
Q3. Do you believe that God has a plan for your life?[9]

And the unavoidable answers being:
1. **YES**
2. **NO**
3. **YES**

Which then leads to one last obvious response — that of:

Asking God to show you what to do next.

By now you would have figured out that I like to think a bit outside the box—or in this case *INSIDE THE BUBBLE!*

I suggest that even God likes to use prayer bubbles! He will do whatever it takes to get your attention. James 4:8 reminds us to come close to Him and He will come close to us.

Chapter Eight

I SEE YOU

In the movie 'Avatar'[10], the phrase "I see you" impacted me deeply with regards to the sanctity of life— whether animal, human … or avatar. Having worked as a Primary School chaplain for a number of years, "I see you" took on a very different meaning, as I would literally "see" hundreds of people—children, parents and teachers—everyday. But did I really 'see them'? Did I really see them as individuals created by God—unique, valuable, precious—each with individual needs and feelings?

The above thoughts came to me in the middle of the night a while ago as I lay there half asleep, I needed to get up and write them down—but why, I was not sure.

There is probably a whole other book(s) to be written on the "I see you" phrase, but as soon as my conscious mind became fully awake, my thinking took a different path. It turned from perception of the physical and spiritual kind to hearing perception.

How many times have you had a conversation with someone and one of you have used the phrase "I hear what you are saying"? Of course, I recognise that on occasions the one using that phrase may simply be trying to appease the other.

CHAPTER EIGHT

"I hear you" came to me in stark contrast to "I see you". The latter being an expression of true recognition of the person as a living soul—with all their uniqueness, qualities and flaws. "I hear you" is different, in that for a person without any hearing impairment i.e. normal hearing, we hear sounds and voices 24/7—yes, even when we are asleep.

Medical research in the area of palliative care reveals that our hearing is actually the last of our senses to remain active in the final dying stage of life. Highlighting for us the importance of speaking words of affirmation to our loved ones who are in palliative care or in a comatose state. Also reinforcing that any conversation being had around the bedside should not be argumentative or negatively disparaging. Hearing therefore, is a gift-sense that sustains life.

This has also jolted my thoughts to highlight the importance of praying over children when they are asleep in the form of positive declaration of their preciousness in God's eyes as well as the delivering prayers over sickness, depressions, rejection and trauma. I would encourage all God-fearing parents and grandparents to engage in this sleep time prayer scenario over their children and grandchildren. My wife and I have seen miraculous turnarounds in our children's peer relationships, behaviours and attitudes as well as physical health as a result of praying audibly over our children sleeping in the growing up years—even teen years!

But hearing is not just a special gift for the dying, it is indeed a precious gift for the living. Ask any hearing-impaired person i.e. someone who has suffered hearing loss over time or was born with some hearing loss as distinct from someone who was born deaf. A person who has lost their ability to hear knows only too well the frustration of losing their ability to communicate clearly particularly in group settings or crowds.

As a hearing-impaired person myself, it is important for me to point out here that I have not lost my ability to speak! Note to the reader: *please consider your hearing-impaired family and friends ... 'see' them by all means but also make sure that they 'hear you'.*

My awakening thoughts have certainly taken me much further than anticipated. Not only is it paramount that we 'see' others, but it is also even more important that we 'hear' them. What are they really saying? Especially when the right words just won't come, even for a well-articulated person—beneath their wordsmithing speech—what are they actually trying to communicate, or deny? You know quite well that they are making clever use of words to avoid facing a certain situation.

If we think we know *all* there is to know, then we already know everything we're ever *going* to know. In order to break out of the box, we must begin by asking the right questions. British screenwriter Sir Antony Jay said, 'The uncreative mind can spot wrong answers, but it takes a creative mind to spot wrong questions.' Wrong questions halt the process of creative thinking. They send one down the same old path. In order to change one's life, one must change one's thinking. That means we must be willing to ask these two questions: 'Why must it always be done this way? Is there a better way?' [11]

Now all this talk about hearing has got me thinking more specifically about the listening/hearing process within our brains. We hear sounds and words ... high-low pitch ... fast-slow ... sharp-smooth ... loud-soft ... long-short and so on.

CHAPTER EIGHT

Many of these sounds form language which our brains process into thoughts from which concepts are formed which in turn develop into understanding. And of course—all of which occurs in continual/rapid succession at micro speed. After which, we reverse the process as we attempt to reciprocate our understanding back into concepts through words as we respond to the other person. Of course, in a lecture or meeting or church or performance this is not the case—as we need the capacity to also store the sound information being processed in our brains.

By now you might be wondering where I am going with all this—especially as this is meant to be a book about prayer, right!? As the subtitle suggests: *'turning thoughts into prayer for the prayer hesitant'*, the previous paragraph provides a perfect segue. We all have understanding—some more than others. We all have thoughts and concepts without our minds.

I want to suggest to you that prayer in itself is not a human construct. It is first and foremost a God-given gift—a divine line of communication installed from the beginning. If prayer is talking to God, then Genesis 1:26 makes clear that even the Godhead communicated ... Yes the Trinity—Father, Son and Spirit—had a conversation! *"Let us make man in our image"*. God made man and breathed His Spirit of life into him. God spoke directly to the man Adam, and gave him instructions about his stewardship of the creation. The man responded in obedience, by naming all the livestock, birds, and all the beasts of the fields (Gen 2:20).

Then after God had created the woman, the man spoke in verse 2:23 "This is bone of my bone and flesh of my flesh; she shall be called woman, for she was taken out of man".

Note: the man spoke words!
Question: *Who taught the man to speak language?*

Then in Genesis chapter 3, we read about the man and woman's conversation with the serpent, and then again later in the same chapter another conversation with God. Now if we accept the basic concept that prayer is conversation between humans and God, then we also need to consider these first conversations documented in scripture. Whatever form the conversations took—either vocal communication or dare I say telepathically—it was God's idea. However, because of 'the fall', this divine line of communication was hacked—corrupted—with the virus of sin.

The good news of course is that after thousands of years, we have a virus protection—a malware cleaner—through the life, death and resurrection of Jesus Christ. And ever since the first Pentecost Sunday after the ascension, we now have access directly to the throne of God's grace once again through the Holy Spirit who has re-opened the direct line of communication for all who believe.

In the next chapter we will explore further what 'I hear you' now means for the believer.

Chapter Nine

I HEAR YOU

Yesterday, my wife was talking to a friend on the phone. At one stage I heard her say, "I hear what you are saying!" What did she mean by that statement, I wondered? Maybe she wanted to affirm her friend's conversation—even though she may have disagreed with her friend's reasoning. Or maybe she wanted to acknowledge that she actually understood where her friend was coming from, and so was in agreement.

I also wonder just how often do we actually say, "I hear you!" during the course of our daily conversations? And what do we mean by that?

Applying these thoughts to the process of prayer—and by that I am referring to Biblical prayer—as opposed to religious, secular or magical incantation type prayers. Biblical based prayer that holds to the belief in an all-powerful, all-knowing, ever-present God who sees you and hears you.

As the Psalmist constantly cried out to the Lord to listen to his cry, and by faith in God's faithfulness, ended up reassuring himself that God does indeed hear when we call out to Him (Ps 86:1-10). So, at the risk of prolonging this train of thought that God—the creator, sustainer and giver of life—actually 'hears', let me move on to what I sense is the flip side of the prayer bubble, and that is facing the reality of whether or not we can truly say in response to God: " *Yes Lord, I hear what You are saying!"*

For a hearing-impaired person like me—bombarded by amplified, unfiltered sounds through hearing-aids—this is even more of a challenge. My brain has to work overtime, compensating for missed high-pitch, soft sounds such as 's' and 'f'. As well as differentiating between sharper sounds like 't' and 'k'. Then to also filter background noises or other people's voices and the vocal melodic nuances of the other person with whom I trying to listen to in larger group settings.

There have been many times I have had to turn my hearing aids down or simply remove myself from noisy situations—physically, mentally and emotionally—a constant challenge. No wonder, that I prefer one-on-one conversations or small group settings.

In everyday conversations with my wife, it is a constant challenge—especially as we spend so much time together in retirement—to say, "I hear you. I hear what you are saying." Is that sufficient—it's good—but is it enough? Not really, because almost every time my wife will come back to me and say, "Ok, tell me what I just said!" WHAM!! So many times I am caught off guard.

As a believer and follower of Jesus, I am constantly putting things to the Lord i.e. turning my thoughts into prayer bubbles. I know that He hears me. The challenge on the other hand is … do I hear Him? Do I actually hear what His response to my bubble-prayer is? Or do I fake it?

CHAPTER NINE

What have you been crying out to God for—audibly, or silently? What requests or needs have you sought His provision for? Do you have family member or a friend you continuously bring before the Father who is struggling in some way—maybe with health issues or through a broken relationship? Just as Bob Beaudine reminds us:

- *Nothing takes God by surprise*
- *Nothing is too big for God to handle*
- *God has a plan and purpose for your life through this.*
- *Our response: "Lord, what do you want me to do?"*[9]

When you turn on your radio—what do you hear? Music, talk-back, podcasts, news, weather reports or maybe white noise. The truth is ... even before you turned on your radio those sounds were already being beamed through the bands of radio waves—and you just happened to 'tune in'. But even still ... by tuning in ... did you still hear? Perhaps a better question might be: *'are you listening?'*

Of course you hear—but do you in fact listen? When we say, "I hear you", perhaps it should also mean that we are listening and want to understand what the other person is saying.

Winding up this chapter, I suggest that we short-change ourselves and our prayer life ... yes even short-changing God by not acknowledging firstly that He is actually speaking to us all the time. And secondly, that we do not listen to what He is saying. I will even go further by stating that we dishonour the

PRAYER BUBBLES

Lord by tuning out—blocking out—filtering out what we simply do not want to hear.

We constantly need reminding just like the Israelites did, that God does hear us and He answers—but do we listen?

> [19] People of Zion, who live in Jerusalem, you won't weep anymore. When you cry out to the LORD for help, he will have mercy on you. *As soon as he hears you, he'll answer you.* [20] He might treat you like prisoners. You might eat the bread of trouble. You might drink the water of suffering. But he will be your Teacher. He won't hide himself anymore. You will see him with your own eyes. [21] *You will hear your Teacher's voice behind you. You will hear it* whether you turn to the right or the left. It will say, "Here is the path I want you to take. So walk on it."
>
> Isaiah 30:19-21
New International Reader's Version
Italics added

Pray—not just until God hears you ... but until you listen to God.

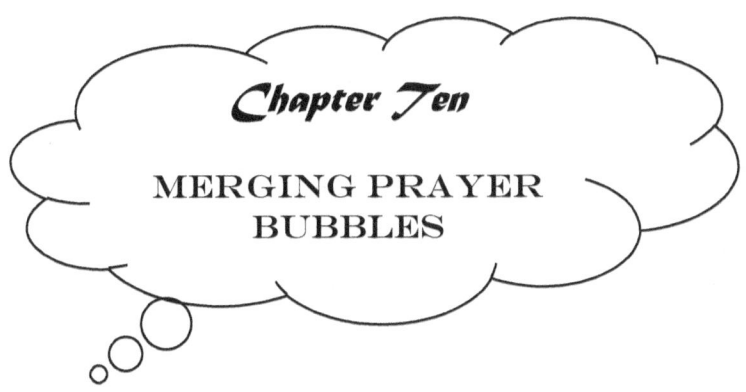

Chapter Ten

MERGING PRAYER BUBBLES

As this book is entitled *'Prayer Bubbles'*, I would like to expand on some thoughts presented in my previous book.

Bubbles are fluid ... not static ... they move ... they float ... they rise and fall ... they drift ... they group and gather.

Have you ever watched someone who is blowing bubbles? I love watching those master gigantic bubble blowers. Have you seen how the bubbles interact with each other? Sometimes the bubbles act like magnets attracting other bubbles which latch onto each other. Sometimes the bubbles touch and burst; and occasionally they will merge to become a much larger bubble.

Rarely, one might even be engulfed by another bubble and yet survive—providing a bubble within a bubble. Unless of course you are a master bubble blower with the skill to create that type of thing.

Prayer bubbles in the same way are fluid—not static ... they too move ... they float ... they rise and fall ... they drift ... they group and gather.

When someone prays in isolation, it's as if they form their own prayer bubble. When two or three people pray together, it does not necessarily imply that they pray within the same prayer bubble. By this, I mean that they may each form their own prayer bubble, which may or may not connect with the others—particularly if they are praying independently without 'hearing' what the others are praying or what the Lord is saying in response. There are times when these prayers do connect and form a cluster—which is naturally and supernaturally more robust. Each person may pray individually about different issues of concern as in 'sentence prayers' or 'leap frog prayers'. Or alternatively, they will 'piggy-back' onto to other's prayers and form a stronger, more unified unit of worshipful, intercessory prayer. [1]

On other occasions, when a few people come together with one particular prayer need and focus specifically staying on task; then it is as if they form one larger bubble of faith in unified strength which is not impacted by individuality. I have experienced this many times over many years, from praying with one person to a group of four or five. Not so long ago, I was with a group of friends who were interceding for someone following an accident. The spiritual energy of faith and unity in the Spirit was palpable.

Dear reader, I encourage you to pray with others — 'leapfrog prayers' and 'piggyback prayers', which in the Spirit strengthen and support each other. Look for—desire those special prayer bubbles which encompass others in which there are no hidden agendas or hobbyhorses. Always strive for unity of purpose and faith. This is even more noteworthy when people from different streams—branches of the Christian faith expression can come together. In chapter 32 of my previous book, I highlight this when *'there were Pentecostals, Baptists, Anglicans, Churches of Christ, Uniting, Presbyterians and*

CHAPTER TEN

Charismatics. And yes ... remarkable as it may sound ... we all prayed together in the unity of the Spirit.' [1]

How good and pleasant it is when brothers live together in unity! (Psalm 133:1)

Be prepared to have others join your prayer bubble by praying in such a way that is invitational and inclusive, and do not hesitate to join other's prayer bubbles. Even individual bubbles in the natural realm can flow in the same direction!

One last cautionary thought on this matter of joining prayer bubbles: be careful not to override someone else's prayer in a way that might make them feel inadequate. Let your prayers be full of grace. If you feel that you might to add further depth to someone else's prayer, then consider stopping and asking their permission to go deeper with them.

Finally, how would you include someone in a prayer bubble who is not a believer or a sceptic without forcing the issue? In other words, what do you do when you ask someone if they would like you to pray for them and they appear wary or uncertain? After all, one key component of this book is about 'prayer hesitants' ... right?! Their hesitation may be that they would feel awkward or embarrassed or that they don't actually want you to pray right there and then.

When I was a school chaplain, I made this offer many times and learnt quickly through the prompting of the Spirit, to qualify my invitation to say something like: *"That's ok. But I do want you to know that when you leave this space, I will say a prayer for you. Is it ok with you if I share with you what I will be praying?"* I never once had anyone say that they did not want to hear. So, I would then proceed to explain in simple terms the type of prayer that would be relevant to their situation. On, each and every occasion, that person would smile and say thank you. Some even went as far as saying *"that's exactly spot on!"* In that regard, I would take that as *'AMEN'*.

It is always such a privilege to invite someone into a space of moving forward in their faith journey.

Prayer bubbles are fluid ...
    they too move ...
        they float ...
            they rise and fall ...
                they drift ...
                    they group and gather ...
and they *burst!*

Chapter Eleven

'INNIE' OR 'OUTIE'

Are you an 'innie' or an 'outie'? And no, I am not talking about belly buttons! I am actually referring to introverts and extroverts.

An introvert is not so much a shy person, but rather one who finds their re-charge more in solitude, unlike an extrovert who is usually more loud and out there—as one who draws their energy from being with and around other people.

Have you ever wondered about the different ways introverts and extroverts engage in prayer? Introverts have a greater tendency towards contemplative-reflective type prayer. Whereas extroverts find it much harder to be reflective or even sitting or standing still for that matter—let alone remain quiet!

From my observation, praying out loud, in simple terms seems to come more naturally to extroverts—but the caution for them is to not pray out loud just for the sake of being heard (by God or others). Remember, God looks on the heart (1 Samuel 16:7).

Introverts, on the other hand, appreciate solitude ... silence ... the flicker of a candle and maybe some contemplative

CHAPTER ELEVEN

music. They may even appreciate the opportunity to write and/or draw, or even the use of icons. A cautionary word here though when using symbols, icons and objects such as candles, pictures, statues, crosses or even beads. The commandments are very clear when it comes to worshipping any graven image. We are not to pray to objects made with hands—but to the Lord Himself—to the God who created everything. These icons and objects do not hold any special power—they are simply meant to enhance our focus ... not to become our primary focal point.

The thing is, whether you are an 'innie' or 'outie', there is neither a right way nor a wrong way to pray. JUST PRAY ... out loud ... in silence ... by yourself ... with others ... for others. The Apostle Paul urged the people at Ephesus to 'pray in the Spirit on all occasions with all kinds of prayers and requests' (Ephesians 6:18). Such good advice.

Pause and ponder here for the moment: what are the sorts of prayers and setting where you feel most alive spiritually—more intimate with the Lord? Let me encourage you to create those spaces—cultivate them—making time in your prayer life for them.[12]

Regardless of whether one is an 'innie' or an 'outie', even though we know we should pray, there are often times when we find it difficult to do so. Eliot Kern has even suggested that despite having a clear incentive to pray, we may still find it 'unnatural.'[13] On the basis of what I have written previously, 'unnatural' is an interesting choice of word. I guess other ways of saying this might be 'foreign' or maybe even 'a conversation with a language barrier'. After all, the wisest man of the Old Testament, wrote "God has put eternity into the heart of man."

(Ecc 3:11) And so with that premise in mind, prayer should be as natural as breathing.

[Eliot Kern is a content producer/writer for Eternity New s published in Australia]

I can pronounce a few words in Thai e.g. *Sawasdee, hong nam chai, mai pen rai*—but other than that, Thai is a foreign language to me. However, as far as prayer is concerned, as long as we have breath … we *can* pray. The challenge for us then, is not so much that prayer is 'unnatural' but rather one of neglect. Neglecting to make prayer part of our daily routine, is as if we are cutting off our oxygen pipeline to heaven.

Kern also suggests—as do I suspect—that 'we neglect prayer at least partly, because unlike much of our daily activity, it doesn't produce anything *instantly*.' No wonder, we actually question—does prayer really make a difference? He also likens prayer to 'donating to a charity', as he questions, "does prayer bring about change 'out there' in the world or even change within ourselves?" [13]

So, whether one is an 'innie' or an 'outie', let us consider for a while the matter of processing. We all process things differently. For me, I process things more internally even before I can put pen to paper—let alone speak it out—regardless of whether it's in the area of finance, home maintenance, planning for an event or even praying.

My wife, on the other hand—and I suspect most females—tend to process their thoughts into spoken words. To balance this out fairly, I have worked with a number of males who are very much external processors. It seems they can't help themselves—they just have to talk things out as they process their thoughts.

CHAPTER ELEVEN

I am fascinated—and frustrated at times—when during a conversation, my wife can be talking about one thing, and then as she sees or hears something which has caught her attention, in the course of what was a normal conversation she simply keeps talking but now she includes what she has seen or heard, and then without even taking a breath she will go back to talking about what she had been saying being before distracted!

This of course highlights just how easy it is for any of us to be distracted in our prayer-thoughts. It is a constant challenge to stay focused and on task in prayer! I dare say, some people might brush this off by declaring that 'the devil is trying to distract us.' Whilst that may be true in part, my estimate through experience, is that it is more often our own wandering thoughts which distract us in our prayer times.

Handwriting has become for me, a vehicle for internal processing over many years of journalling, and in more recent years of being an author. For me to go straight to the computer and just type away my thoughts … is a great challenge. I find that I need the intermediary phase of processing of handwriting before externalising my thoughts through the keyboard onto the screen. Although this is not always the case.

So what about internalising or externalising when it comes to prayer? Great question. Being an internal processor does not mean that one is necessarily quietly unopinionated or slow. It just means that you require some space as well as time—often alone—in order to get clear on how you are feeling and what you need to do. And then, once you have figured it out, then you might even become talkative or even opinionated!

In a similar way, prayer for internal processors, requires time and space—often alone and in silence. Sometimes journaling, sometimes either reading scripture or a reflective piece of writing. The most important ingredients are silence and solitude ... for it is in the silence that the Lord speaks—direction is given—answers are received—the unclear becomes clear—unrest finds its calm. For some internal processors, they may also find that including some visible or tangible enhancers such as a candle, sand, music or water may assist in their processing.

Internal processing is critical when one has a lot going on in one's mind. Maybe a huge decision to make ... or a major health issue to face ... or having a strong emotional reaction such as being overwhelmed with other things going on in your life. We are more likely to turn inwards—into our own thoughts and emotions—rather than reaching outwards to people in our life, in order to gain clarity. These are also the most opportune times to turn one's thoughts into prayer bubbles. Prayer-bubbling consisting of quiet, reflective prayer provides internal processors a very effective method of 'hearing from God'.

Just as there is no 'ideal' processing style, so too there is no 'ideal' method of praying—except to say what works for each individual.

At this point it is incumbent on me to also caution external processors who may be naturally loud or opinionated or simply just super confident—to know that they are not necessarily 100% certain of everything—but to realise their talkativeness might just be having to say something out loud simply because they are still uncertain about how they feel.

CHAPTER ELEVEN

Similarly, external processors need to pray out loud—either by themselves or in a group setting—in order to assist them in processing their pleas and petitions to the Lord.

External processors need to talk things out with the Lord—they need to vocally express their worries ... thoughts ... desires ... hurts and petitions in much the same way as a lawyer might present a defence case.

Which leads us on to acknowledge that Jesus Christ is our advocate at the right hand of Father God. The Holy Spirit carries our thoughts and words in a bubble, so to speak— to Jesus who bursts the bubble and presents our case before the Father's throne. Knowing this, enables us to boldly approach the throne of grace—from a position of victory rather than defeat. And the Father, Son and Spirit know precisely how to process your prayer-thoughts and words. They know exactly what you need in order to receive the processing of your answers.

As I draw this chapter to a close, I am reminded of hearing my daughters calmly saying to their pre-schoolers *"Use your inside voice!"* At that age children are learning about 'inside/outside' voices. Inside voice requires speaking gently and yet loud enough for others to hear. Whilst an outside voice is an expressive way of loud-play-communication.

I must admit that I have on occasion been left flabbergasted in a prayer meeting to hear a normally quietly spoken person virtually yelling even screaming at God. Yes, I agree that people in the group need to hear, but not to the point of feeling uncomfortable due to the volume and intensity of voice projection.

Each person should be encouraged to pray with sincerity and passion without causing discomfort for others present. I want to suggest, that we exercise caution praying in a public space when it comes to raising our voice—as God does not need to be yelled at—He is not deaf! And the Devil does not need yelling at either—just being commanded in Jesus' name.

Conversely to the above scenario, I have observed people who normally would be loud and vocal in conversation, who drop the pitch and volume of their voice, when praying, to an almost inaudible level to others in the group. Maybe it's that they simply feel either embarrassed at praying or inadequate. They may even feel overwhelmed in the presence of God.

it is in the silence ...
that the Lord
... speaks

☙

Chapter Twelve

IN YOUR DREAMS

Dreaming is a strange phenomenon. We all dream. As I dream when I am sleeping, my subconscious mind is aware of what is happening—as well as my physical body like when I go to kick a ball and end up kicking my wife instead! OUCH! Although, my conscious mind has no control over my dreaming thoughts; so too, in a similar way it is when praying in tongues—it is me and the Lord—where my conscious words are put into neutral in order that my spirit allows the Holy Spirit to take the lead.

I am not going to attempt to unpack the theological arguments for and against praying or speaking in tongues here; so if you choose to skip the rest of this chapter … that's ok. However, please do not just put the book down and discount the rest. Let me point out that I am not writing as a biblical scholar, but simply sharing my experiences and observations over many years.

A friend recently asked me what I meant when I talked about 'tongue praying.' My response was to explain that when my rational-conscious mind cannot frame the words for spoken prayer in my native tongue, being filled with the Spirit means

CHAPTER TWELVE

that I have access to one of the gifts of the Spirit that the Apostle Paul addresses in his first letter to the Corinthians. In other words, when English words are inadequate by allowing this gift to operate, I am able to pray in an 'unlearnt language', aka 'an unknown tongue'. *He that speaketh in an unknown tongue edifieth himself* 1 Corinthian 14:4 (KJV)

Praying in tongues in private is distinct from speaking in tongues in a church or small group setting where others hear. The two practices are easily confused, but are as different from each other—like breathing in and breathing out. Just like when I prepare my own breakfast differs from when I have guests and I offer to make them a cappuccino or when my wife prepares a meal for friends. The former is a private matter—the other is to be shared. The Apostle is very clear on this in 1 Corinthians 14: 1-22. Speaking in tongues in a church group setting requires wisdom, sensitivity and respect. It also requires interpretation. If someone speaks in a tongue in a public gathering, that person should seek the permission of the church leadership to bring such—for either that person needs to interpret the message or someone else does. If this does not happen, then the tongue speaker is out of line within the body of believers—and I dare say ... out of sync with the Holy Spirit.

Observations from my personal experience about praying in tongues is that it allows the Spirit to capture my unintelligible words. These He collects as in a bubble and delivers them to Jesus who is at the right hand of the Father interceding for us.

On the other hand, if I speak in a tongue in a public setting, the Spirit captures my unintelligible words which He collects like in a bubble and delivers them to Jesus, who then receives the bubble of words and turns it inside out as it were, then hands it back to the Spirit. The Holy Spirit then hands it back either to me or someone else present—with the interpretation expressed in the common language of the people in order for them to understand and be encouraged.

Now, going back to my dream analogy, sometimes the Lord gives me limited understanding in my awakening period of what my dream was—although it may be disjointed and not fully comprehensible. So too, neither praying in tongues nor speaking in tongues were ever intended to be nightmarish or disturbing, but edifying to the individual as well as the church.

So, as we draw this chapter to a close, let me encourage you—challenge you—to go back and reread the whole of first Corinthians chapter 14. Read it in several translations or paraphrases, and ask the Holy Spirit to give you understanding.

He collects our prayerful thoughts and carries them in a bubble

Chapter Thirteen
UNSPOKEN PRAYERS

This chapter has been inspired by the writing of Lynn H Pryor. In one of his blog posts he writes about the many occasions, sitting in the circle of a Bible study / Life Group, and as prayer requests were shared, occasionally someone would say, "I have an unspoken prayer request." Or as some people might simply say, "Unspoken."[14]

It's hard to know what to do with that. We become clueless as how to pray. *"God, there's a need out there. I don't know whose it is or what they need, but would you take care of it?"* We're called to come before God boldly and confidently (Heb. 4:16), but it's difficult for us to pray confidently when the request is so vague and we don't even know what we are praying about.

Let's flip the coin and recall having had those moments when someone's name or face comes to mind. You have no idea why, but you sensed a strong, even overwhelming compulsion to pray for that person. Lynn Pryor suggests that it's just like another version of an 'unspoken' prayer request. You felt strongly led to pray for the person by name, but you were clueless as to what to pray. You prayed anyway, standing in the gap for that person. *"Lord, I don't know what this person is facing right now, but strengthen them. Work in their life and let it be obvious that You are at work."*

Although there is a different approach with these 'unspoken' or unknown needs. We *can* learn to pray with boldness and confidence by embracing a prayer Paul prayed for the Ephesian church.

> *"For this reason I kneel before the Father from whom every family in heaven and on earth is named. I pray that he may grant you, according to the riches of his glory, to be strengthened with power in your inner being through his Spirit, and that Christ may dwell in your hearts through faith. I pray that you, being rooted and firmly established in love, may be able to comprehend with all the saints what is the length and width, height and depth of God's love, and to know Christ's love that surpasses knowledge, so that you may be filled with all the fullness of God"* (Eph. 3:14-19).

We may not know specifically how to pray for an individual, but we can pray that the person would "be strengthened with power in their inner being through his Spirit, and that Christ may dwell in their heart through faith." If you know the person is not a believer, then pray they will become one. You want Christ to dwell in their heart! You also want Christ to dwell i.e. be totally at home—in the heart of a believer too. Pray that Christ would strengthen them to live a life that pleases God.

We can also pray the person would be "rooted and firmly established in love." Paul's prayer was not just that the believers would be grounded in God's love, but that they would see just how wide, long, high, and deep His love is. Whether a person is facing something discouraging, debilitating, or

CHAPTER THIRTEEN

difficult, we want them to experience God's loving presence. No matter what they face, nothing will separate them from God and His infinite love for them (Rom. 8:38-39). This is not a prayer just that they would be aware of God's love; it is a prayer that they would be immersed in God's love and experience it deeply.

The phrase Paul used: "to know Christ's love that surpasses knowledge" sounds like an oxymoron. How can we know something that is beyond knowing? Paul's prayer—and mine too—is to know by experience the love of God. We will never fully know and understand that love, but we can still enjoy its benefits. Just as a baby clings to his mother instead of going into the arms of a stranger, despite the fact that the infant doesn't know how much his mother loves him, yet the infant still trusts that love, rests in it, and enjoys it. In the same way, that can be our prayer for others. Whatever a person is facing, they needs God's strength. They need God's presence. They need the comfort, encouragement, and strength that comes from God's love. Let me encourage you to work towards making this a regular prayer. As the names of people come to mind throughout the day, pray for Christ's presence and empowerment in their lives. Pray that the love of God would give them the strength and encouragement they need to stand strong.

even the unheard-of prayer ... is heard ... in heaven

Chapter Fourteen

BUBBLE PRAYERS

The first two of the following prayer-strategy activities were included in my previous book. Each of the activities below can either be employed as part of a Prayer Party or simply as a private form of prayer-meditation.

THOUGHT BUBBLE PRAYERS:[1]

This is a great starter for a Prayer Party.

Provide each person with a bottle of party bubbles

- Each person finds a space by themselves
- Provide each person with a small bottle of party bubbles
- Use the Bubble Blower to blow some bubbles
- As you blow bubbles—consciously release the thoughts, the stresses, the anxieties, worries you have come with today —name them—speak them off
- Watch them POP and disappear—as they disappear give thanks to the Lord *"Lord Jesus I release [NAME IT ... anxiety, anger, confusion, fear etc.] into Your hands. Thank you Jesus"*
- Pray: *"Fill my heart with Your love. Fill my mind with Your thoughts with power and peace."*

CHAPTER FOURTEEN

- Once you have released these things to the Lord, allow Him to change your thought bubbles into Praise Bubbles: BLOW BUBBLES of PRAISE. *Praise Him for His faithfulness, His mercy, His protection, His provision, His healing, His presence.*
- When you hear "*Oh Lord, hear our prayers*" please return to the circle / sit breathe / relax.

FLOATING PRAYER[1]

- A reflective activity, a suitable conclusion to a Prayer Party
- Provide each person with a black bean, a chickpea and a pumpkin seed (mothballs are also very affective)
- Provide each person a glass filled with SODA WATER
- Identify which of the objects represents you
- One by one drop each of the objects into the water
- Do not hold the glass—place it on the table
- In your own space … sit, stand or kneel and watch silently
- Observe what happens
- Allow the Lord to speak to you personally in this space about yourself, your prayer life about other matters regarding the ups and downs of life
- Be sensitive of others in this space—stay calm and please restrict your movement
- Please do not talk to anyone around you

When you hear "*Oh Lord, hear our prayers and thank you for your answers*" finish up and return to the circle.

PRAYER BUBBLES

BAUBLE PRAYERS

- Provide a large fruit bowl filled with large clear plastic baubles which contains a small, coloured sheet of paper (colours of fruit)
- Each person takes a bauble
- They open their bauble and take out the piece of paper then ...
- Write a specific prayer for someone ... a leader ... a volunteer ... a teacher ... a family member ... someone in need ... yourself ... your church etc.
- Be as specific as you can ... as this prayer request will not be made public—it can also be anonymous if you so desire
- Place your written prayer back into the plastic bauble and then ...
- Everyone finds a space to sit, kneel or stand ...
- Hold their prayer bauble ... holding the bauble as if offering it to the Lord
- Pause and pray over this silently and intentionally ...
- Then take the bauble and place it back into the large glass fruit bowl you took it from originally
- Wait until others have also put their bauble back in to the bowl ...
- Then without rushing, take one of the other baubles. Hold it—**do not open it!**
- Prayerfully lift this bauble prayer before the Lord—keeping in mind that the Lord knows exactly what this prayer request is about. (this is another example of 'Unspoken Prayers' from the previous chapter)

CHAPTER FOURTEEN

- Respectfully and reverently return the bauble to the fruit bowl and choose another
- Repeat the silent-prayer-process and return the bauble to the fruit bowl.

When you hear *"Oh Lord, hear our prayers and thank you for your answers"* finish up and return to the circle.

BALLOON-BUBBLE PRAYERS:

OPTION #1

- Provide each person with a balloon, felt tip pen and paper about post-it note size
- Each person is asked to draw a speech-thought bubble on the paper and then to write anonymously their specific fears ... doubts ... rebellious actions/attitudes ... disappointments ... abuse ... anger ... etc.
- Place the paper into the balloon and blow up the balloon, tie it off then ...
- Place the balloon in the centre of the room
- Once all the balloons are in the centre, each person is to take a balloon at random then pop the balloon either with a pin or by sitting or standing on it to make it burst
- Collect the pieces of paper and place them either in a rubbish bin or a large pot to be set alight
- Light the papers ... as the fire is burning the group stands around the pot and prays either out loud or

silently intentionally renouncing the hold of these written confessions

OPTION #2

- Alternatively to writing on paper ... give each person a permanent marker with which to write on the balloon.
- Writing fears, anxieties, doubts, disappointments etc.
- The balloons are blown up and placed in the centre of the room and burst at random.
- Once all the balloons have been burst, the remnants are gathered into a pile
- The group stands around the pile and prays either out loud or silently intentionally renouncing the hold of these written confessions
- The pile can then be disposed of as trash.

Chapter Fifteen

OPEN-ENDED BUBBLES

Take a breath. Be aware of the Lord's presence.

Now once again I ask the same question as last time: *"How does one bring closure to a book such as this?"*

Same answer: *"You don't! You leave it open-ended."*

And if you simply close the book and say, *"Well that didn't help!"* then I am sorry. I propose that by leaving an open-ended parting, it's a bit like saying *"Come back again!"*

You can literally close this book and walk away unchallenged and unchanged; or you can leave the book open and refer back to it from time to time for a pick-me-up challenge or reminder. Keep this book handy like you would a photobook or album on the coffee table. Flip through the pages occasionally and take a breath and allow your thoughts to be formed into prayer bubbles.

PRAYER BUBBLES

My prayer is that you will have come to realise that there is no absolute right or wrong way to pray—other than to pray!

In fact, I pray that you embrace the many different forms or praying. I pray that it order for us to move forward spiritually we take a step of faith in the direction we need to go. And that just like when we are blowing bubbles, you will discover your prayers can go forwards, upwards, downwards, sideways or even backwards—all under the whispery breath of the Holy Spirit. Amen.

Oh and finally, remember that eventually all those prayer bubbles will burst. So, go on … blow some bubbles.

Prayer bubbles …
*going **up** and **down***

Sources & Quotes

1. Gary B Lewis, *Vertically Challenged: the ups and downs of praying* (Self-Published, Australia, 2020)
2. https://movies.disney.com/the-misadventures-of-merlin-jones
3. https://en.wikipedia.org/wiki/The_Chrysalids
4. https://www.cnet.com/science/scientists-have-found-a-way-to-convert-thoughts-into-speech/
5. A A Milne, *Winnie-the-Pooh*
6. Strongs Bible Concordance, https://eliyah.com/lexicon.html
7. https://hymnary.org/hymn/OTR1950/89
8. https://www.dictionary.com
9. Bob Beaudine, *2 CHAIRS:the secret that changes everything* (Worthy Publishing, NY,2016)
10. https://en.wikipedia.org/wiki/Avatar_(2009_film)
11. https://vision.org.au/the-word-for-today/daily-reading. May 15, 2023
12. https://www.24-7prayer.com/the-introvert-at-prayer/
13. Eliot Kern, https://www.eternitynews.com.au/good-news/does-prayer-make-a-difference/
14. Lynn H Pryor, https://lynnhpryor.com/2022/07/28/how-to-pray-for-someone-when-you-dont-know-what-to-pray/

Other sources not quoted

- https://faithhealth.org/prayer-bubble/
- https://en.wikipedia.org/wiki/Telepathy
- https://faithhealth.org/prayer-bubble/

 Gary Lewis is a retired Primary School Chaplain and mentor to School Chaplains. His background is Primary School education, Children's Ministry, and Church Pastor covering more than 50 years of ministry. His extensive lay ministry has also included Worship Leading, Preaching, Prayer Ministry Coordinator and Church eldership over many years.

His previous book *Vertically Challenged: the ups and downs of praying* was published in 2022. He has also authored several children's books — picture story books and novels—all of which are based on true stories from his chaplaincy work with primary-aged students. In addition, he has also sharing stories through being a blogger for more than fifteen years https://life-markers.blogspot.com/

Gary's books are available at:

https://www.garylewisbooks.com/

www.ingramcontent.com/pod-product-compliance
Lightning Source LLC
Chambersburg PA
CBHW030303010526
44107CB00053B/1798